FIGHTER PILOT

LIFE AT THE
EDGE

STEPHEN RICHARD

Ransom

Wings.

Cockpit.

Air intakes.

Fighter Pilot

by Stephen Rickard

Published by Ransom Publishing Ltd.
51 Southgate Street, Winchester, Hampshire SO23 9EH
www.ransom.co.uk

ISBN   978 184167 758 3

First published in 2010

Copyright © 2010 Ransom Publishing Ltd.

All photographs courtesy US Air Force.

A CIP catalogue record of this book is available from the British Library.

The right of Stephen Rickard to be identified as the author of this Work has been asserted by him in accordance with sections 77 and 78 of the Copyright, Design and Patents Act 1988.

THE F-22 RAPTOR

Engines.

F-22 RAPTOR DATA

Length:	19.90 metres
Wingspan:	13.56 metres
Height:	5.08 metres
Top speed:	Mach 2.25 (1,500 mph)
Acceleration:	*TOP SECRET*
Max altitude:	60,000 feet
Cost:	US$ 143 million (each)

This is my aircraft.

It is an F-22 Raptor. It is the best fighter aircraft in the world.

Today is a test flight.

First, the aircraft must be checked before take-off.

The weapons must be checked, too.

Then the Raptor is filled up with fuel.

I move the aircraft onto the runway.

I am ready for take-off.

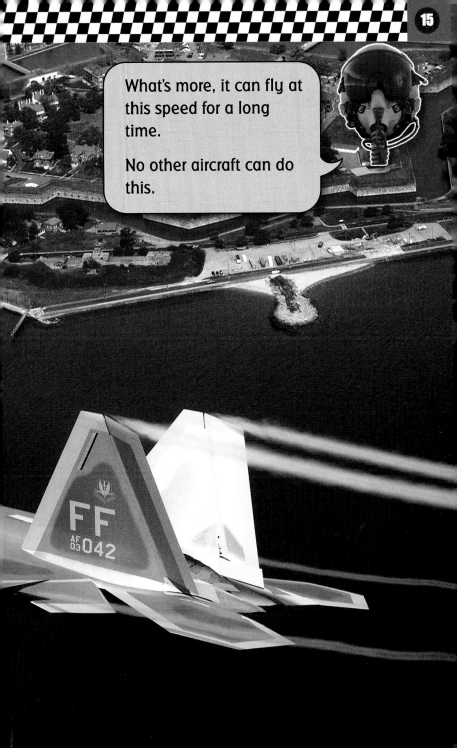

The Raptor is also hard to see on radar. So enemy aircaft cannot spot it.

The Raptor is a stealth aircraft.

It also has special paint. This helps make it hard to see on enemy radar.

Not long ago somebody scratched the paint on a Raptor. It cost about one million dollars to paint it again.

The Raptor can go faster if it uses afterburners.

This is when extra fuel goes into the engine.

But the extra heat from the engines can be seen on radar.

So there is a price to pay.

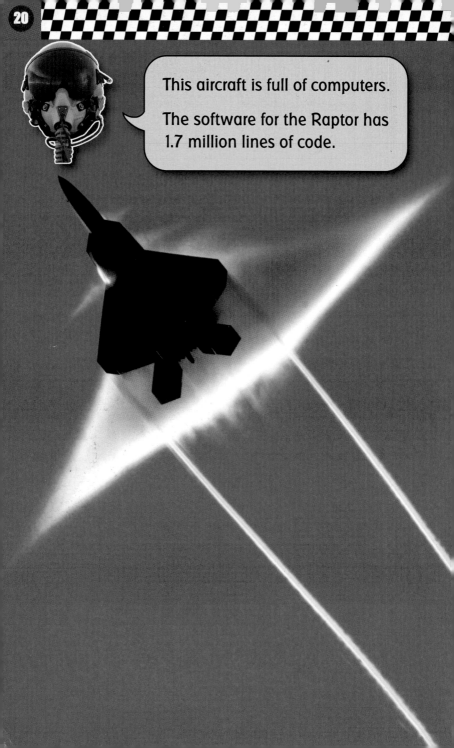

If there is a bug in the software, the Raptor might crash.

We say 'First look, first shot, first kill'.

This means that if an aircraft sees an enemy aircraft first ...

... it can fire the first shot.

And if you fire the first shot, you can destroy that aircraft.

So we must see the enemy first.

The Raptor can see enemy aircraft before they can see it.

In the cockpit, I am in control.

But I don't see all the information.

I don't have time to see everything. This aircraft is too fast.

So the Raptor only tells me important stuff.

Like problems ...

... and other aircraft.

It shows enemy aircraft as red circles on my computer screen. Friendly aircraft are green triangles.

If it's not sure - they are yellow squares.

Sometimes we fly with other aircraft.

These two Raptors are flying with a B-2 Stealth Bomber.

If a Raptor runs out of fuel, it can get more fuel in the air.

This Raptor is getting fuel from a KC-135 Stratotanker.

The F-22 Raptor is a fighter aircraft.

It can carry air to air missiles as well as bombs.

It has six AIM-120C
'Slammer' missiles
and two AIM-9
'Sidewinder' missiles.

G forces happen when an aircraft turns very quickly.

The Raptor can make forces up to 9G.

That is OK for the Raptor, but 9G can kill me.

I must be careful.

But this is my job.

So tomorrow I get to do it all over again!

How good is that?

JARGON BUSTER

acceleration
afterburners
altitude
dogfight
flares
G force
IFE – In-flight
   emergency
Infra-red heat seekers
Mach

NVG – Night vision
   goggles
radar
Raptor
starboard
stealth
Stratotanker
supersonic
UFD – Up-front
   display